PACK UP AND PAINT
Waterscapes

Tom Robb

Stoddart

First published in 1988 by
Stoddart Publishing Co. Limited
34 Lesmill Road
Toronto, Canada
M3B 2T6

Canadian Cataloguing in Publication Data

Robb, Tom
  Pack up and paint waterscapes

(Pack up and paint series)
Includes index.
ISBN 0-7737-5176-9

1. Marina painting – Technique.
I. Title.   II. Series.

ND1370.R62 1988   751.4   C88-093108-6

Printed and bound in Belgium by Offset-Printing van den Bossche

Introduction

The very essence of water must surely be opposed to the fundamental concepts of painting. It seldom has any colour of its own, reflecting everything above and beneath it. It is almost impossible to find it absolutely still, so your picture keeps changing all the time. And when it falls from the sky, it has a habit of permeating everything with a luminous edge – very difficult indeed to capture in pigment and paper.

And yet I believe that there is almost nothing in my experience that can be more satisfying and fulfilling than a river estuary, with its misty banks and boat traffic of all kinds.

Landscapes, too, can be enriched by an appreciation of how to paint water. Mill pools, docklands and even swimming pools offer endless possibilities for the painter who wants to combine land and water subjects.

In this handbook you can begin with a few pebbles in a stream and go on to a wide vista of sand and shoreline. I've added some mountains and harbours for holiday painting; simple wave patterns in monochrome for making useful studies – everything, I hope, that will convince you that working on waterscapes must be the finest reward of all for your efforts to *Pack Up and Paint.*

Tom Robb

Contents

Why waterscapes?

Water is unique. It embodies movement and transparency in a way that nothing else we paint can ever do. For many people it has all kinds of symbolic meanings and philosophical accoutrements.

As anyone can see from the subjects I choose to paint most often, I have a special affection for waterscapes. In addition to the challenge of working on as elusive a subject as water itself, there is always something interesting to observe: plants and small fish in a little pool, making curious shadows; brightly dressed people with glowing skins lying conveniently still on deckchairs and towels; the simple shapes of boats in a harbour, and the complicated shapes of their tackle.

Not surprisingly, we carry experience with us from early childhood. Ducks in the bathtub lead on to sandy beaches; to holidays by a river; to a lake to sail across in a small boat . . .

This is a subject in which there must surely be something for everyone. The beginner can simply enjoy the tremendous appeal of water in all its forms, stunned perhaps by the variety of surrounding material. Water in still ponds; water in fast-running streams; narrow, winding rivers; broad, limitless oceans. Sandy shores, mud banks, cliffs, thick vegetation. All express their watery setting in some way.

The second stage is to home in on some particular form of water that attracts you. The use of reflections; the action of waves; the colours of the surface; the constantly changing shore scoured by tides; the reaction to weather and light. Experience will help you to sort out why one kind of picture is easier in watercolour than in oil, and vice versa.

The third approach, as always, aims to turn the painter into an artist – in this instance, one of a long tradition that includes great innovators such as Turner and other masters of classical marine paintings.

Any of these approaches is valid, and all three can be used at different times to give variety and excitement to your adventure.

Practical planning

What you will need

Obviously, the first consideration is how to cope with water. Somehow the best views always seem to be from the most inaccessible places – the middle of the pond, the steep bank of the river, the farthest point of the jetty.

Let's look at a really watery site first. I love to paint from a boat, even better, actually standing in the water. I found a wonderful pair of fisherman's tall boots that are perfect for all-year painting, although I have to admit that on warm spring and summer days they are uncomfortably hot. Then I switch to ordinary calf-high rubber boots. Make sure you buy the kind with good gripping soles, not one of the too-fashionable styles with smooth soles.

Even in the hottest weather, when standing up to your knees in cool water is a consummation devoutly to be wished, you must have something on your feet. River beds are strewn with rocks, mud, gravel, old tins and bits of glass; as you step back to check your horizon, it's all too easy to fall and injure yourself. Remember that blood red is not a colour that occurs too often in waterscapes.

Carrying your gear out into the water is the next problem. Again, the fisherman came to the rescue with a multi-pocketed jacket in waterproof canvas. Try to find one with the biggest possible pockets, deep rather than wide, so that pencils, charcoal and so on won't slip out.

The fisherman's typical basket, made of heavy, tough wickerwork, is another aid. It should be large enough so that you can pack your lunch (and even a folding fishing rod if you are going to catch your own), as well as an oilskin bag to hold a few rags and perhaps a towel for the inevitable, though always unexpected, bath.

An easel is essential, and if you are not walking far, get the heaviest portable model you can find. Running water has surprising power, and the light aluminium easels that are so useful for outdoor painting in other circumstances simply will not stand up to the current; even when bolstered by rock and gravel piles around each leg, they are likely to slip and collapse.

These light models aren't much good in a boat either, they can be tipped over by the wind, or by ripples in the water. It is better to take a table easel, only a few feet high, which you can set up firmly; keep the legs steady with a few round balls of putty or clay pressed tightly around each foot, and then pressed down against the deck.

A hat keeps out the worst of the sun or rain, and an umbrella is useful against too much of either.

Where to go

Choosing your site is one of the most enjoyable parts of planning your trip. Waterscapes offer an incredible variety of places and unusual views. Think about your most accessible beach or harbour jetty, for instance. There are some unusual ideas on pages 16-19.

But remember that water is all around us, too, and often close to home. Lakes can be forgotten by painters unless they are wide and surrounded by beautiful landscapes. Small lakes also provide many different subjects: reed beds, rocky shores, clear pools, rippling surfaces.

Brooks and creeks, too, are often ignored, but they also offer wonderful waterscapes, full of interest: a meandering shore line; exciting patterns made by shallow areas with rock formations; rich undergrowth and plant life along the banks. There are often small breaks in the water-level, with cascades and flecks of white water where the current runs fastest – the perfect test for your skill in using white.

For a complete contrast, have a look at swimming pools. Artificial linings give remarkable colour tones to the water. Lane markings are fun to do as exercises in the reflective effect – watch as the reflections break up after swimmers go past.

Any place with tides can be rewarding. As the land is covered, and the level rises and falls, there are fascinating changes at mill ponds, locks, canal gates, dry docks.

If all else fails, you can often find water where water doesn't necessarily belong. Think of lovely shimmering pools and puddles when it rains; streaky windows as the storm throws sheets of water down along the panes.

Even a country horse trough can reflect the sky in a special and beautiful way.

Here are two possible places where you might decide to go. Work out what you want to learn from the outing and how you can best adapt – both medium and mood – to the place and time you have chosen.

Setting up

Each medium has its own application to painting
waterscapes. You must, for instance, always take the weather
into account when you plan your outing.

If it's a warm spring or summer day, I always prefer
watercolour. The washes dry so quickly that I can do two or
even three paintings at once, layer by layer. The paper stays
pleasantly stiff and easy to handle. And on the beach, any
sand or debris blown onto the surface can be brushed off
easily as soon as the painting is dry.

There are many kinds of light easels that work well when
they do not have to actually stand in the water; most are
aluminium, and their legs can be hammered into the soft
sand or soil banks at the water's edge.

Do remember, if you are working near salt water, *never* to
fill your water bottle from the sea. It will destroy many
pigments, and turn others into crusty layers which continue
to show through no matter what you do.

Oil paints are really responsive to the hand when I am
attempting to create sketchy landscapes that include water
in the view, as in this study of a river estuary, or when I want
to fill the canvas with stormy scenes and flecks of foaming
waves.

But oil-painting equipment is usually bulkier than watercolour, and you'll need a little more protection to keep pigments, palette and rags from getting damp. Even on shore, I find that a waterproof box is good for storage, preferably one with a cover that I can close when the spray is particularly heavy.

Rocky sites are full of convenient crevices and niches to support the easel legs, and the rocks themselves provide a flat table for your working gear. Although sand makes setting up easy, I avoid painting with oils anywhere near the beach; there is too much wind, and it blows a fine cover over the surface of the painting very quickly – and very immovably.

Drawing is a good choice for working near water; you need only a few pencils or some chalk and a pad. And you can find a seat anywhere. But I take the precaution of not keeping my drawing sticks in my pocket; if I forget, and lean over to look at something from a slightly different angle, everything falls out into the mud or the water.

Choosing what to paint

You've found an unusual site; you've laid out your materials, and now you need to focus on what you are going to paint.

A river bank: the silhouettes of fishermen and the strong vertical lines of the reed bed cry out for drawing in pen and ink or watercolour. You should be looking for contrasting shapes and directions and for the surface markings which give the impression of running water. A ragged edge will suffice for the foreground.

If you are lucky enough to find a picturesque place like the village pond and house, you have the makings of a lovely composition. Work in watercolour or oil, trying slightly different viewpoints, with the house bulking on the right, the skyline travelling down to the distant trees or bushes on the left.

The pond itself makes the central focus; and remember, you don't need to include the whole shape. Reflections are important because in calm weather they provide the picture with a double subject, above and below the line of the pond.

The city scene offers still another challenge: an urban setting, the composition far more informal than in the landscape, dominated by the paired buildings, but with the rainwater shimmering on the pavements. I tried this in heavy oil impasto for an impressionistic effect.

Finally, you have a tight geometric pattern made by the rectangular pool and its surrounding paving, all angles.

Four different approaches to waterscapes, each with its special quality, each a lesson in creating an interesting picture from a simple scene.

Finding something different

Harbours

I find harbours and boats endlessly fascinating as subjects, offering a wealth of interest and a variety of approaches. Because I paint them so often, it was difficult to pick out one project as an example of something different, but this watercolour of the corner of a marina is one of my favourites. I used the shapes and colours to create a semi-abstract impression of the buildings and boats.

Working early in the morning is best before there are too many sailors and fishermen about to block your view. If you can, try to paint it in this style of flat blocks of colour in the morning; then go back and paint it in tones in the afternoon. Making this sort of double approach will teach you a great deal about the basic structure of the objects you look at.

Boats

A close-up of one of the boats in the harbour picture on the previous page shows how much there is to look at in a busy harbour or marina. And how many ways you can practise changing your approach to learn something new each time.

The small sailing yacht had been put onto props so that the hull could be cleaned, ready for the summer ahead. This gave me an opportunity to see the whole shape of the bottom instead of just the part you normally see above the water. Working only in black and white also made it a good exercise in creating the effect of a rounded deck without using colour.

The painting of the entire harbour on the previous page was done early in the morning (and I do mean early – at five a.m. on a midsummer day to catch the best light and the quietest time); the tone sketch on the opposite page was painted late that same evening, with the light slanting low on the horizon to give me the strong shadows that bleached out colour.

Tones are very important to the artist; they are the vocabulary of shape and dimension which has nothing to do with colour.

If you find it difficult to separate the concept of tone from the colours you know are there, try letting the sun do the work for you. Late in the day, or even at night, you'll find that the colour has dimmed so much that you actually see only blacks and greys, so it simply becomes a matter of painting what your eyes show you.

You can also work in any single colour; it doesn't have to be black. Try using sienna or even red, adding plenty of water. When you use watercolour, always put down the lightest washes first; then add the middle tones, and put the darkest tone on top. With oils, you start the other way, first painting the darkest tones, adding the middle and finishing with the lightest.

The four seasons colour codes

It may be difficult to imagine that water itself has seasonal colours, but looking closely at waterscapes throughout the year will show how much the colours that you use should change, not only with the weather and the climate, but with the month as well.

On the opposite page I have made a quick comparison of the way water will adapt to the climate and the colours of the sky, from spring on the top through summer, winter and autumn. I've based these little squares on years of experience, but you should try to see the differences for yourself.

Find a bit of water nearby, where you will be painting quite often during the course of the year. It needn't be the seaside; any creek or river bank will do. But for this exercise, don't use a swimming pool; the bright colours on the bottom distort the way the water reflects the atmosphere.

Because you want a glimpse of sky, work from a distance. If you try to look at water too close up, you won't be able to see the variations that the seasons create.

Make a note of where you are, then visit the same spot every month, even if it is only for a five-minute sketch. Keep a sheet of paper for all twelve squares, so that you can compare them easily when you have finished.

You need only a few inches of water to see how much the reflections change over the year. If you are ambitious, make your squares each time in watercolours, in pastels and in oils, next to each other. That will give you a comparison between the mediums as well as the subject.

Working with these colour codes throughout the year will show you how to capture the atmosphere of place and time in paint, and help you to recognize very small gradations in the mixes.

They also show how you can use just a few tubes or pans of pigment to create an entire palette. Most amateurs use far too many colours when mixing their paints, and end up with muddy tones. It is never necessary to mix more than three different colours.

The spring palette

Spring colours are seen not only in the clear water, but in the yellow-green of new leaves at the water's edge, and in the soft colours of the trees and hills beyond the lake.

The blue sky is a special colour – vibrant and clear, yet still soft in the fairly gentle light. This is often repeated in the violet-blue shadows on the houses and waterside buildings. All the colours have a great deal of yellow in them – even the reds and browns. The following colour code uses oil paints, above, and watercolour, below. Because the washes are so light we have given an idea of the ratios of pigment to water, but you should try to work out your own proportions.

Viridian green 2 Zinc white 2	Lemon yellow 1 Cerulean blue 3	Alizarin crimson 1 Titanium white 3	Viridian green 1 Lemon yellow 3	Olive green 2 Lemon yellow 2
Lemon yellow 2 Burnt sienna 2	Viridian green 2 Lemon yellow 2	Lemon yellow 1 Viridian green 3	Lemon yellow 2 Zinc white 2	Ivory black 1 Titanium white 3
Raw umber 1 Zinc white 3	Yellow ochre	Yellow ochre 2 Titanium white 2	Cerulean blue 1 Lemon yellow 1 Zinc white 2	Cerulean blue 1 Ivory black 1 Zinc white 2
Cobalt blue 2 Zinc white 2	Yellow ochre 2 Olive green 2	Cerulean blue 1 Zinc white 3	Cobalt blue 1 Zinc white 3	Raw umber 3 Zinc white 1
Alizarin crimson 1 Wash 3	Raw sienna 2 Wash 2	Burnt sienna 1 Wash 3	Olive green 1 Wash 3	Cadmium yellow 2 Wash 2
Viridian green 3 Wash 1	Viridian green 3 Cerulean blue 1	Lemon yellow	Raw umber 1 Wash 3	Cerulean blue 1 Wash 3
Ivory black 2 Wash 2	Lemon yellow 3 Cerulean blue 1	Cobalt blue 1 Wash 3	Prussian blue 1 Wash 3	Lemon yellow 3 Ivory black 1
Cadmium red 1 Lemon yellow 3	Alizarin crimson 2 Wash 2	Cobalt blue 1 Lemon yellow 3	Cadmium red 1 Wash 3	Ultramarine blue 2 Wash 2

The summer palette

A beach is the perfect place to look at the summer palette of waterscapes. The sun reflects off the sand to give sparkle and clarity to all the colours, and the light in the sky makes the sea very bright.

With landscapes in the summer, you'll find the palette rich and deep, but at the beach or near a large body of water the light keeps the colours clear and even a little bleached. Avoid any tinge of grey in the mixtures; you may find it useful not to use black at all. Make your colours stronger by using undiluted pigment instead.

The following colour code uses oil paints, above, and watercolour, below.

Cobalt blue 3 Zinc white 1	Lemon yellow 1 Viridian green 1 Zinc white 2	Lemon yellow 1 Olive green 1 Zinc white 2	Cobalt blue 1 Titanium white 3	Prussian blue 2 Cerulean blue 2
Viridian green 2 Cerulean blue 2	Ultramarine blue	Cerulean blue 3 Zinc white 1	Ultramarine blue 3 Titanium white 1	Cerulean blue 2 Zinc white 2
Ivory black 1 Zinc white 3	Cadmium yellow 3 Cobalt blue 1	Lemon yellow 1 Prussian blue 1 Zinc white 2	Viridian green 3 Titanium white 1	Cadmium orange 3 Yellow ochre 1
Ivory black 2 Zinc white 2	Ivory black 3 Cerulean blue 1	Ultramarine blue	Prussian blue	Viridian green 1 Zinc white 3
Yellow ochre 3 Mauve 1	Prussian blue 3 Cadmium red 1	Cerulean blue 2 Cadmium red 2	Ultramarine blue 3 Cadmium red 1	Cobalt blue Ivory black
Ultramarine blue	Prussian blue	Cerulean blue 2 Alizarin crimson 2	Cerulean blue	Ivory black
Cerulean blue 1 Lemon yellow 3	Alizarin crimson	Ultramarine blue	Indian red 3 Burnt umber 1	Alizarin crimson Wash
Mauve	Cerulean blue 3 Mauve 1	Viridian green	Lemon yellow 3 Viridian green 1	Cerulean blue 1 Viridian green 3

The autumn palette

Here you can see just how the landscape employs the darker, richer colours of autumn, and turns the water the same deep tones of the autumn palette. The bleaching effect of light at the seaside has gone, and the reds and browns of the trees are intensified.

Even the white sails only serve to point up the brilliant colours of the scene. Flecks of white foam on water would serve just as well.

Oil paint always seems to me appropriate for this time of year, no matter where I am painting out of doors. There is something about its texture and solidity that suits the season. This little sketch is in oil, but the colour code shows you can achieve the same effect in other mediums.

The autumn sky is deep blue, without any yellow or grey. Of course, when it's rainy it won't look like this, but the brilliantly blue skies of sunny autumn days are particularly crisp and inviting. So that is when I choose to paint most often. And of course that same blue is reflected in the water.

Look for purples and reds, deep browns and dark greens. There is still relatively little black in the mixtures. You will find warm colours most appropriate, even though the weather is growing cold.

I like to use oil, in lovely thick chunks, during autumn, working with a palette knife or one of the larger brushes. This allows me to reinforce the richness of colour by adding to the texture, moulding the shapes in broad areas, and creating shadows and hollows in the surface.

As the year gets colder, so my paint becomes flatter! Think of the late autumn landscapes in gold and brown which traditional painters worked on in the nineteenth century. They used thin layers of oil as glazes, one on top of the other.

I find myself using that technique more and more often as the season progresses. The colours grow quieter and the brushwork much finer, until autumn turns finally to the cool colours of winter.

The following colour code uses watercolour, above, and pastels, below.

Raw umber 1 Ivory black 1 Wash 2	Viridian green 2	Indian red 2 Raw sienna 2	Viridian green 3 Ivory black 1	Cerulean blue 2
Cerulean blue 1 Ivory black 3	Burnt sienna	Ivory black	Cobalt blue 2 Ivory black 2	Raw umber
Alizarin crimson	Lemon yellow 1 Cobalt blue 3	Burnt sienna	Ultramarine blue 3 Raw umber 1	Burnt umber
Ivory black	Ultramarine blue 3 Alizarin crimson 1	Prussian blue	Prussian blue 2 Lemon yellow 2	Ultramarine blue
Bright blue	Mauve	Light brown	Red ochre	Turquoise
Yellow ochre	Light sky blue	Red brown	Deep green	Leaf green
Spring green	Sea green	Pale ochre	Dark grey	Vandyke brown
Purple 1 Brown 3	Sky blue	Bright green	Burnt sienna	Moss green, deep

The winter palette

When winter comes, the water takes on the cold tints of the surrounding landscape and the grey colours of the winter sky. Even on a sunny day, the blue is likely to be tinged with grey, and this is reflected in the water below.

I chose this particular watercolour to show something of the winter palette, just because the water is mostly mud. That is appropriate to outdoor painting once the autumn has turned into winter's cold and bleak chill; even the sea will be the same mud-grey.

Painting water-saturated ground is much more difficult than painting clear water, and keeping the effect of still water in the bottom of the channel wasn't at all easy. I used a flat wash without any shadows, and it shows how all the rich summer and autumn colours have become muted and pallid.

The blacks you use now should be ivory, and the blended colours full of black browns rather than red browns.

Rocky promontories and jetties by the sea are also fine subjects for winter waterscapes. Painting them – or anything else out of doors now – can be cold and uncomfortable, but the season brings startling changes to our preconceptions of 'blue' water. You'll find grey, brown and occasional green tones in the water, but seldom clear blue. Even on a bright sunny day in winter, the sea looks cold.

Winter is also the time when the bare bones of a picture become very clear: without the lush growth of trees or the sparkle of summer sun and flowers, everything seems to take on a stark, almost gloomy, appearance. A painting in tones of grey would probably look very realistic, almost as if it were in full colour. On the other hand, there are wonderful and delicate pale colours which you could never see during summer, or at any time when the sun was strong enough to saturate the scene with its own light. These pale pinks, blues and lilacs only come into their own now.

Try painting the same scene at different times of the year, but especially once in winter and once in summer; you'll be startled by the subtle changes in what you see.

The following colour code uses pastels, above, and watercolour, below.

Pale blue	Viridian green	Blue-green	Light purple	Sky blue
Light pink	Sap green	Middle grey	Sea green	Light mauve
Prussian blue	Cerulean blue	Deep olive green	Sky blue, light	Deep pink
Black	Ultramarine blue	Leaf green	Blue-grey	Yellow green
Cobalt blue 3 Viridian green 1	Alizarin crimson 3 Ultramarine blue 1	Yellow ochre	Sky blue 2 Mid-grey 2	Cerulean blue 1 Viridian green 3
Alizarin crimson 1 Wash 3	Cerulean blue 1 Wash 3	Ultramarine blue 2 Wash 2	Ultramarine blue, deep	Viridian green 3 Prussian blue 1
Ivory black 1 Wash 3	Cerulean blue 3 Cadmium red 1	Ivory black 3 Burnt umber 1	Cerulean blue 1 Ivory black 3	Prussian blue 1 Wash 3
Viridian green 2 Wash 2	Viridian green 1 Wash 3	Cobalt blue ½ Wash 3½	Ivory black 3 Wash 1	Lemon yellow 1 Ivory black 3

Special problems

Sand and beaches

Beaches, a favourite summer-time playground, are also fine places in which to capture the special appeal of the sea. So beach scenes give the painter a bonus: a day of enjoyment, plus the chance to produce a delightful waterscape.

But they present a few problems, too. The wide horizontal lines of the sand and the water's edge can create a visual emptiness. And if you back off to include more of the beach, as well as a good stretch of the water itself in your scene, the foreground is likely to be filled with a featureless desert of beige.

Because the sun is high in the sky, it bleaches out the colour and takes away many of the shadows that make objects and shapes interesting. All conspire to flatten your scene, and leave it blank and boring.

There are a number of ways to change it all. First, move your viewing card about to take in some natural feature that will make its own vertical statement. In this particular beach scene, there was a convenient cliff rising just to the right; but if it hadn't been there I could easily have invented it. A building of some sort would do as well – or a stand of trees.

Then search for something on the beach that will make a
good spot of colour or add interesting shapes and textures
to the scene.

I was lucky here, for there were a few families picnicking by
the water. I moved in fairly close so that the forms of the
grown-ups, sitting watching the children playing in the
water, created not only an interesting break in the
horizontal line of the water's edge, but gave me a
diminishing scale, adding the space and dimension usually
created by shadows. The fishing rods that the children had
temporarily abandoned provided an extra – and helpful –
vertical line.

The strong colour contrast came from the series of
windbreaks they had set up to shelter their deck-chairs from
the wind. The bright stripes were a marvellous exclamation
point, and I have put them into other paintings many times
since, whenever I needed a splash of something yellow or
green on the beach.

Cliffs and mountains

Strictly speaking, rocky promontories are more often a
problem of landscape than of waterscape, but they often
confront you when you're painting on lakes and rivers or
looking back towards the shore from a boat or a pier. They
can dominate your picture, sometimes almost to the
exclusion of the water. You can either let them do so,
making them the strong, positive focus as I did here. Or you
can treat them negatively, moving far enough away so that
they become merely a distant line on the horizon.

If you are going to take the positive approach, find an
interesting combination of outlines for the skyline. Look for
the natural fault lines and variations in the surface that will
give you dimension and scale; painted in broad strokes, the
effect is considerable.

Techniques

Moving water

Making water move is probably the single most difficult technique that the waterscape painter has to develop. Still water, with its quiet surface, is relatively straightforward; by careful observation of colour and shadow, you can create quite remarkable effects. But moving water seems to be so hard to capture in the medium of paint that it fazes many otherwise competent artists.

As with all techniques, the simplest is the best. Start with a piece of pastel, a pen or charcoal. Sit down in front of running water and see how you can make the lines move.

Begin with something easy like a waterfall, where you can see the strong vertical lines created as the water tumbles over the edge. It's like a series of pleats in a dress. Remember not to make the verticals too regular or too continuous down the slope. Add a bubbly doodle or two and – hey presto! – a waterfall.

Now find something a little harder – horizontal ripples. A rocky stream bed is ideal; the shapes of the rocks give you something to draw around, to show how the current flows.

This stream looks very much like a Japanese gravel garden which has been raked to resemble flowing water. And that's a good clue. If you are really out of luck in finding the right kind of stream, you can make yourself a little model with sand, a few rocks, and a rake to draw patterns in the sand to make it look like water.

Another vertical current – this time at the edge of the sea where the incoming tide breaks up in small, foaming waves. Concentrate on the difference between the tidal water running in, flat and strong, and the bubbly effect of the foam where it curls over the sand.

Finally, slowly moving water – the most difficult of all to draw. The patterns are wide and meandering, the patches not only bigger, but wider, near the front of the drawing, growing narrower and thinner as they retreat into the distance.

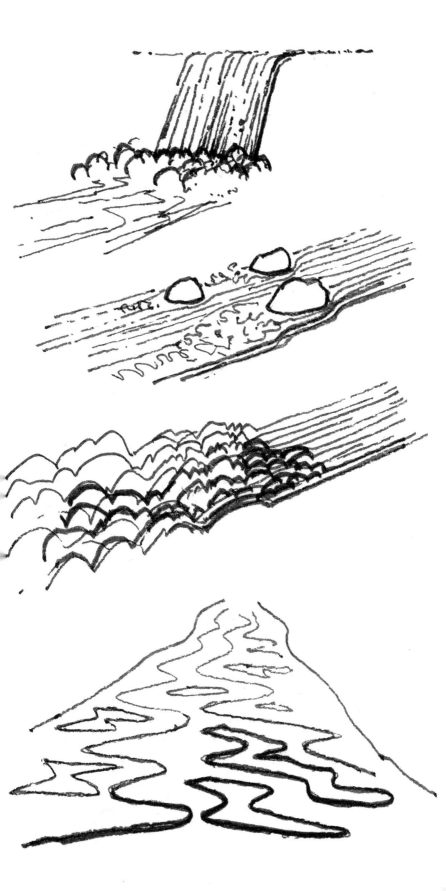

Wave patterns in tone

Here are examples of how to practise with tone instead of thin line. Use pastel, chalk or charcoal, drawing in monochrome and letting the paper work for you with white.

Begin at the sea's edge. You want to take a viewpoint that is slightly away from you towards the open sea. Look for the movements of waves up and down. Try to capture the broad sweep of the waves rather than the details of the currents as you did in the previous project.

Then concentrate on the sea where it meets the shore – where the waves break up in foam on the beach or on the rocks. Work in broad strokes, letting them be the current, rather than drawing it in lines.

Now lie down and see what the water looks like on the horizon. There should be patterns of waves like the little peaks of a child's drawing. As with so many naïve conceptions, the peaks actually work for the artist, so long as they are not too regular; you need stretches of line, as well, to make the illusion complete.

Finally, move away from the water so that there is some sort of foreground. In this case, I was drawing from just behind a few sand dunes, their little tufts of grass making a vertical pattern to give the horizontal line of the water that much more emphasis.

Remember that you are looking for the irregular pattern. Breaking up the line is much the most effective way of achieving the impression of movement.

Try to do this kind of sketching as often as possible. Aside from making special trips, you can practise with any nearby body of water. Even water running into your bath or from the tap in the garden can give you a good opportunity to sketch. But bear in mind the inevitable, impending water shortage: keep the tap running only when you are going to use the water – to irrigate the garden, for instance.

Special notes

One, two, three

For sketching out of doors, a single tube of paint would be quite adequate, and two could be considered a luxury.

The little study above, of two fishermen, was done quickly with just a little blue, thinned down for the washes on the heads and legs.

On the opposite page, above, a smudge of green has been added, and below, various washes of green and blue were combined to make a complete riverside scene.

So you need never use the excuse that you didn't want to carry a heavy box of painting equipment – a brush, a tube and a plastic bottle of water fit neatly into the smallest pocket.

And if you are really looking for the minimum weight, ask a chemist for one of those trial sizes of new shampoos or colognes. After their contents are used up, they make perfect water-carriers for a short expedition out of the office on a hot summer's day. Some hotels leave tiny bottles of soap and shampoo in their guests' rooms; make friends with a travelling colleague, and you can be equipped for life.

Reflections

Here is a feast for the waterscape artist, with reflections of an entire city street reproduced in remarkable detail by the still water of a canal. I have to admit at once that this is not Venice. It's a street by an ordinary industrial canal, but the problems and the approaches are exactly the same.

In a way a scene like this is actually two scenes, one above the water, one below. It used to be said that classical painters in Venice finished the scene above the water first, then turned their canvases upside down and simply painted the scene again. When this was almost dry, a quick rub up and down created just a few deviations to make it look like reflections. Turn the canvas right side up again, and you had a perfect painting, the two scenes indeed matched and mirroring each other.

That pleasant trick is certainly still possible with oil paints, and if you want an afternoon's enjoyment, you might try it yourself. However, it is no substitute for accurate observation. And unless the water is absolutely still, the reflection will never be as mirror-perfect as that trick would make it appear.

You have to train your eye to work below the surface, so to speak. The reflections will usually be moving slightly; even if the water is still, the clouds move, and this creates all sorts of ripples in the water image.

Follow the traditional technique part of the way by painting the image above the waterline first. That will give you a base. Then block in the ragged edges of the reflected buildings. Add the windows or any other details. Keep your wrist flexible and use a dry brush to break up the lines.

When you begin to paint reflections, choose a place where the water is relatively quiet, so that you don't have to cope with too many currents and surface ripples. A canal lock is ideal, but even a large puddle in the rain can make the most unprepossessing building look like Venice.

Close-ups: below the surface

Sometimes any kind of waterscape can seem overwhelming
– those wide horizons, the endless sea stretching out
beneath a similarly endless sky. The very grandeur of
mountains and lakes can have an inhibiting effect. So I need
to break off for an hour or two and re-focus on something
pleasantly containable – right, so to speak, underneath my
feet.

The translucency of water gives us an added dimension.
Although, looking from an angle, the surface seems to be
solid, just one glance straight down reveals an entire world
of shapes and shadows.

Here I have sketched two fish; the first is swimming in
deeper water than the other, so that all you see is a dark
shadow. Since you want to give the impression of
something hovering between the background and the
surface, wash the paper first with a palish blue (or green or
violet, or whatever colour you want the water to be).

When the wash is dry, paint your fish quickly with a few
strokes; then let that dry, too. Finally, add a top wash and
you'll be surprised to see how the fish seems suspended in
the medium.

The second fish is swimming in shallow water. The shadow
is created by the sun, which also catches the ripples on the
surface and produces moving shadows over the entire
picture.

You can repeat the same sequence by painting the seabed
first with a plain wash, then adding the fish and the shadow.
But this time don't wait until it is bone-dry before you wash
in the surface. You'll want to lift off enough paint from the
dark fish to keep your ripples light, and it's easier to do that
right away, with a damp rag or a sponge.

When you are lifting off an uneven shape, always do it with
quick flicks to make sure that your edges aren't too regular.

Close-ups: bird's eye view

In tropical climates or near the shores of clear unpolluted lakes, we can easily see many things: coral shells; sea plants of all kinds; tiny jelly-fish and other strange creatures; brilliantly coloured rocks. But even in the muddiest waters under cloudy skies, there are countless interesting things to paint.

Here I've shown just some of the ways you can learn to look beneath your feet to find fascinating shapes and colours. The gravel or pebbled sand, above, where the water breaks is enormously complex, and makes a delightful study.

Look at how the pebbles change from the dryer surface of those in front to the ones beneath the water. Just a thin line of white separates the two. You'll never be able to work standing up at an easel, so find a low chair, a convenient jetty or a flat boulder. You may need to adjust your position to see the difference between the pebbles clearly. I have students who crouch right down, but that's too uncomfortable for me! In any case, I find that getting too near is almost as bad as being too far away; I can't see the variations in colour nearly so well.

A good way to learn to paint small things effectively is to make a seaside still life. Only a few pebbles of different colours and shapes will do nicely. The group of seven, below, displayed a whole vocabulary of rock surfaces in just a few inches.

Such an exercise is especially useful on a cloudy or foggy day, but it is just as much fun any time your eyes need a rest from the glare of the horizon.

Concentrate carefully on each pebble, comparing it with the others. Don't try to paint one alone; your eye needs help in making judgements about what it sees – that one is redder; that one is mottled; that one is perfectly round . . .

Take your time, too. Even though it seems a simple task, these seven pebbles took me three hours to do.

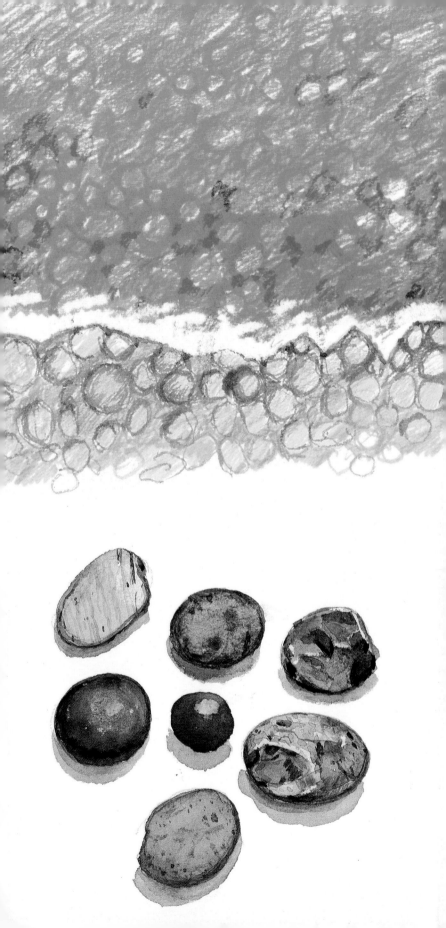

Not a boat in sight

Just in case you should think that all my waterscapes are
filled with boats, here is a sketch I made in the
Mediterranean with nothing but the shore, the reed beds,
the sea and the sky.

You can be even more single-minded than this. Look at the
seascape on pages 6 and 7, where there is absolutely
nothing but the sea. However, I think that it is usually more
interesting to include something else, to create a focus for
the eye.

In this sketch, I worked from a low position next to a cove. I
wanted the line of reeds to stretch entirely across the paper,
and, as you can see, I succeeded in that respect.

But the outing was a salutary lesson in practical planning.
On my first trip to the coast, I lost two pairs of boots in the
squelchy reed-bed mud; got soaked through as the moisture
seeped into my cotton clothes, and was badly cut and
scratched by the sharp edges of the reeds.

The next visit was an entirely different matter. I brought
along an inflatable boat, a long stake, a piece of rope and an
old pair of driving gloves. Once I had floated out in my boat
to the right place, I pushed in the stake, tethered the boat,
and painted away for the whole afternoon in dry comfort.

A first approach:
modelling with colour

After you have been painting out of doors for a while, it makes a lot of sense to give yourself a challenge. Trying to meet a specific goal can only increase your ability and set you on the path to achieving something worthwhile.

However, it's just as foolish to attempt too much as it is to stop trying at all. If these are your first real outdoor expeditions, concentrate on creating patterns or designs that will help you later when you attempt grander work, but which will, in the meantime, also be enjoyable and amusing in themselves.

Here are two wave patterns in colour. Unlike the little pen drawings earlier in the book, these both depend entirely on colour for their effect.

The top pattern was painted looking straight down at the water in a fairly quiet swimming pool, with some ripples but no continuous current. The bright colour was, of course, the reflection from the tiled lining, and the passing swimmers set up a kind of lace design on the surface.

Try not to paint at indoor pools; their colour is quite different from those out of doors, and the lighting may make it difficult to see the surface patterns distinctly. However, if that is all you can find, work from as high up as possible – standing, or from a tall stool.

The darker waves, below, were painted from a dock, and on a dark and windy day when the water looked heavy, almost greasy, with no feeling of translucency at all. The waves rolling into the shore on my left had a strong vertical movement, and looked as though they were made of thick cake icing or modelling clay.

Do a number of studies for yourself on different days, so that you have a variety of shapes, designs and colours. This will give you a glimpse of how much there is to find in just one aspect of waterscapes. Keep the studies pinned up around your working place at home and, every time you go out, make another design of the water surface, no matter what else you bring back.

Eventually you should have an extremely useful diary.

A second approach: stormy seas

We've been looking at waterscapes in reasonably good weather. However, it would be a great mistake to ignore the magnificent wild excitement of stormy seas, when the rocks are awash with spray and the very air seems tossed about by the ocean.

Once you have become comfortable with your outdoor equipment, and have tried different ideas and mediums, it is time to give yourself a stormy project – but a project where you can enjoy the visual excitement without too many hazards. It isn't a good idea to wait until nature obliges with a tornado.

Look for the effect rather than the exact situation, say, a bit of rocky coast that is easily accessible, and where you can organize a safe seat for yourself and your equipment. Near a lighthouse is ideal, on an outcrop, which makes a convenient studio.

You want to be just above the tide level, and preferably near enough to the rocks below you to see the spray and the foaming white water of the waves. The lower your eye level, the larger and bolder the spray will appear in your finished painting.

You must be safely settled on the rock before you begin to paint. Make sure you have checked the tides; and start to work when they are going out rather than coming in. Sometimes you can get so caught up in what you're doing that you forget to look at your watch. Take an alarm with you and set it for a good half-hour before the time that the nearby rocks will be flooded. And make sure you know exactly how to get back to dry land!

Work as quickly as you can. You want the feeling of motion and excitement, not a finished study of precise lines. Oil makes a good medium; it shows depth and movement in the brush-strokes.

And always, please, be careful! Water is a marvellous subject, but, in quantity, it must be treated with respect. Don't take chances with your safety, forcing someone else to have to rescue you.

A third approach:
holiday memories

Your first real challenge comes when you choose a broad
subject, and make the effort to produce a large painting.
Being on holiday gives you the time, the space and the
attention span for working seriously, and holiday resorts, of
course, are usually picturesque, a word that is almost a
synonym for 'paintable'.

The subject itself doesn't matter, but try to find somewhere
that has at least some of the conditions that you have
described in your sketches of beaches, boats and so on.
You're now going to put to use the skills you acquired in
making them – reflections, boat shapes, sea or lake colours,
the sky. And you will combine them with a feeling for
composition and effect.

Take as much time as you want. Make sure you choose a
comfortable spot where you won't be disturbed too much.
Early in the morning is best at any resort. Although the
evening sun is often spectacular, the whole world will seem
to pass by and make comments on your work – not always
complimentary, and sometimes downright discouraging,
especially if you are only getting started.

This will be an important step for you. Don't rush, but set
yourself some sort of time limit. Perhaps it will be only a
day, perhaps until the end of your holiday. What matters
most is the effort you make, the care and attention you give
to your work. That is how painters become artists.

Going home

After you have finished your first waterscape outings, you need to make an assessment of what you have done. Ask yourself, honestly, if you are pleased with the results.

It's not a question of whether or not you have painted great pictures; for most of us, that comes seldom enough. It is more basic: whether or not you have learned something about your craft, something about the special techniques of painting water, something about your approach to painting, and, above all, what you can do to improve both your skill and your attitude.

No matter what you want out of painting, it is capable of giving you something in return. But it is up to you to decide what that something is.

Waterscapes are especially adaptable to any approach, because there is such fantastic variety. But you mustn't let the subject, for all its beauty, become so all-consuming that you never learn anything that you can use in another kind of painting. That's one way to forget everything.

So when you come home after a trip, while you have a cup of tea, unpack and clean your equipment, keep half an eye on the work you have brought back with you. It's a common axiom that it is hard to look at your own work critically, but if you are to be any kind of painter, self-judgement is absolutely essential to your progress.

Try to assess precisely what you have achieved. Maybe you have learned a little more about how the sun cuts through the water and leaves a trace of golden haze in the blue. Or perhaps it is the contrast between an autumn lake, all dark blues and deep greens, and a winter brook, black and cold. Something you hadn't seen before.

It doesn't matter if your painting hasn't really been able to show that yet. You've learned to see. Work at the skills you need to put what you can see onto the paper or canvas, and you're on the way to growing from a painter into an artist.

Index

Page numbers in *italic* refer to captions and illustrations.

Note on colour charts: the guides in this book have been produced within the limitations of four-colour process printing, and therefore cannot reflect the intensity of certain pure pigments.